My Big Backyard

Roadrunners

Lola M. Schaefer

Heinemann Library
Chicago, Illinois

Customer Service 888-454-2279
Visit our website at www.heinemannlibrary.com

Designed by Kim Kovalick, Heinemann Library; Page layout by Que-Net Media
Printed and bound in China by South China Printing Company Limited.
Photo research by Bill Broyles
Edited by Tameika Martin

08 07 06 05 04
10 9 8 7 6 5 4 3 2 1

Library of Congress Cataloging-in-Publication Data
Schaefer, Lola M., 1950-
   Roadrunners / Lola M. Schaefer.
      v. cm. – (My big backyard)
Includes bibliographical references (p.   ).
Contents: Are roadrunners in your backyard? – What are roadrunners? – What do roadrunners look like? – How big are roadrunners? – What do roadrunners feel like? – What do roadrunners eat? – What is something special about roadrunners? – How do roadrunners stay safe? – Are roadrunners dangerous to you?
   ISBN 1-4034-5048-X (hardcover) – ISBN 1-4034-5736-0 (pbk.)
   1. Roadrunner–Juvenile literature. [1. Roadrunner.] I. Title.
   QL696.C83S36 2004
   598.7'4–dc22

                            2003021022

Acknowledgments
The author and publishers are grateful to the following for permission to reproduce copyright material:
p. 4 Wayne Lankinen/DRK Photo; pp. 5, 8, 10, 16 Stephen J. Krasemann/DRK Photo; pp. 6, 22, 24 C. Allan Morgan/DRK Photo; p. 7 Wayne Lynch/DRK Photo; pp. 9, 11, 12, 18 Joe McDonald/DRK Photo; p. 13 Charles Melton/Visuals Unlimited; p. 14 Sid and Shirley Rucker/DRK Photo; p. 15 John Cancalosi/DRK Photo; p. 17 Charlie Ott/Photo Researchers, Inc.; p. 19 Andy Rouse/NHPA; p. 20 Jeremy Woodhouse/Masterfile; p. 21 Gail Shumway/Taxi/Getty Images; p. 23 (t-b) Joe McDonald/DRK Photo, Charles Melton/Visuals Unlimited, C. McIntyre/PhotoLink/Photodisc/Getty Images, Wayne Lynch/DRK Photo, Corbis; back cover (l-r) Joe McDonald/DRK Photo, Wayne Lynch/DRK Photo

Cover photograph by John Cancalosi/DRK Photo

Special thanks to our advisory panel for their help in the preparation of this book:

Eileen Day
Preschool Teacher
Chicago, IL

Kathleen Gilbert
Second Grade Teacher
Round Rock, TX

Sandra Gilbert
Library Media Specialist
Fiest Elementary School
Houston, TX

Jan Gobeille, Kindergarten Teacher
Garfield Elementary
Oakland, CA

Angela Leeper
Educational Consultant
Wake Forest, NC

Pam McDonald
Reading Teacher
Winter Springs, FL

Contents

Some words are shown in bold, **like this.**
You can find them in the picture glossary on page 23.

Are Roadrunners In Your Backyard?

You might see a roadrunner in your backyard.

They live in dry places, like **deserts**.

Roadrunners build **nests** in trees.

They like places with many bushes.

What Are Roadrunners?

feathers

Roadrunners are birds.

Feathers cover their bodies.

Roadrunners are warm-blooded.

Their bodies make heat so they can stay warm wherever they are.

What Do Roadrunners Look Like?

tail

Roadrunners have thin bodies.

They have long tails, too.

Roadrunner **feathers** are black, white, and tan.

Their legs are gray.

How Big Are Roadrunners?

tail

A roadrunner is as long as a loaf of bread.

Half of this length is its tail.

A roadrunner is light.

One could sit on a thin tree branch.

What Do Roadrunners Feel Like?

feathers

beak

Roadrunner **feathers** feel soft.

Their **beaks** are smooth and as hard as wood.

claw

Roadrunner legs feel rough.

Their **claws** are sharp.

What Do Roadrunners Eat?

Roadrunners might look for food in your backyard.

They eat animals and bugs.

Roadrunners like to eat lizards, worms, and mice.

They even eat rattlesnakes!

What Is Something Special About Roadrunners?

Roadrunners do not fly a lot.

They would rather walk or run.

Roadrunners hop from branch to branch to get into their **nests.**

How Do Roadrunners Stay Safe?

Roadrunners stay safe by hiding or running.

They hide in bushes and tall grass.

Roadrunners run when they see danger.

Sometimes they fly away from enemies.

Are Roadrunners Dangerous To You?

Roadrunners are not dangerous.

They do not hurt people.

Roadrunners watch you coming closer.

Then, they run away.

Quiz

What are these roadrunner parts?

Picture Glossary

beak
page 12
the bill of a bird

claw
page 13
a sharp nail on the finger or toe
of an animal

desert
page 4
a dry place

feather
pages 6, 9, 12
the light covering on a bird

nest
pages 5, 17
a shelter made by a bird for its
eggs and babies

Note to Parents and Teachers

Reading for information is an important part of a child's literacy development. Learning begins with a question about something. Help children think of themselves as investigators and researchers by encouraging their questions about the world around them. Each chapter in this book begins with a question. Read the question together. Look at the pictures. Talk about what you think the answer might be. Then read the text to find out if your predictions were correct. Think of other questions you could ask about the topic, and discuss where you might find the answers. Assist children in using the picture glossary and the index to practice new vocabulary and research skills.

! CAUTION: Remind children that it is not a good idea to handle wild animals. Children should wash their hands with soap and water after they touch any animal.

Index

Answers to quiz on page 22

feathers

beak

tail

claws